Contents

Preface 4
Introduction 6
    Why Personal Finance is Personal 6
    The Importance of Focusing on Your Own Financial Journey 6
Chapter 1: The Comparison Trap 7
    How Comparing Yourself to Others Can Derail Your Financial Goals 7
    The Psychology Behind Envy and Financial Insecurity 8
    Case Studies: The Hidden Costs of Keeping Up with the Joneses ..8
Chapter 2: Understanding Your Unique Financial Landscape 9
    Assessing Your Income, Expenses, and Financial Goals 9
    How to Create a Personal Financial Statement 10
    Setting Realistic Financial Goals Based on Your Situation 11
Chapter 3: Building and Sticking to a Budget 12
    The Basics of Budgeting: Creating a Simple, Effective Budget ...13
    Tools and Apps to Help Manage Your Budget 14
    Strategies for Sticking to Your Budget 15
Chapter 4: Smart Spending: Prioritizing Needs vs. Wants 16
    Identifying Essential Expenses vs. Discretionary Spending 16
    The Importance of Mindful Spending 18
    Techniques for Avoiding Impulse Purchases 18
Chapter 5: Saving for the Future 20
    Building an Emergency Fund: Why and How 20
    Strategies for Long-Term Savings and Investments 21

Retirement Planning: Starting Early and Staying Consistent........22

Chapter 6: Navigating Debt and Credit..24

    Understanding Different Types of Debt and Their Impact 24

    Strategies for Managing and Reducing Debt...................................25

    Building and Maintaining Good Credit..26

Chapter 7: The Role of Financial Independence 28

    What Does Financial Independence Mean for You?.....................28

    Steps to Achieve Financial Independence......................................29

    The Importance of Financial Education and Continuous Learning 31

Chapter 8: Developing a Healthy Money Mindset............................32

    Overcoming Financial Stress and Anxiety......................................32

    Cultivating a Positive Relationship with Money............................33

    The Role of Gratitude and Financial Mindfulness 35

Chapter 9: Monitoring and Adjusting Your Financial Plan 36

    Regularly Reviewing and Updating Your Budget..........................36

    Adapting to Life Changes and Financial Shifts..............................37

    When and How to Seek Professional Financial Advice................38

Conclusion: Embracing Your Financial Journey 40

    Embracing Your Financial Journey..40

    Staying Focused on Your Own Goals and Values 41

    The Rewards of Mindful Money Management 41

Appendices 42

    Appendix A: Budgeting Templates and Worksheets 42

    Appendix B: Recommended Financial Tools and Resources 43

    Appendix C: Additional Reading and Educational Resources.......44

Glossary of Financial Terms 46

Preface

Welcome to "Mind Your Own Money: Practical Strategies for Managing Your Finances and Achieving Your Goals." As you embark on this journey through the world of personal finance, I want to share a bit about why I wrote this book and what you can expect to gain from it.

My name is Alphonso Horton, and my journey into the realm of finance has been shaped by both my education and my real-world experiences. Holding an Associate of Arts in Business Administration, a Bachelor of Science in Finance, and a Master of Science in Project Management, I've had the privilege of delving deeply into financial principles and project management strategies. These academic achievements have provided me with a solid foundation, but it's my hands-on experience as a business owner, financial advisor, and tax preparer that has truly enriched my understanding of personal finance.

Throughout my career, I've had the opportunity to work closely with individuals and families, helping them navigate their financial challenges and achieve their goals. In these interactions, a common theme has emerged: the need for practical, straightforward advice that cuts through the noise of financial jargon and focuses on what really matters. This book is my response to that need.

"Mind Your Own Money" is designed to be a practical guide for anyone looking to take control of their finances, regardless of their starting point. Whether you're new to budgeting, seeking to improve your spending habits, or aiming to build a secure financial future, this book provides actionable strategies and clear explanations to help you succeed.

In the chapters ahead, we will explore essential topics such as budgeting, smart spending, saving for the future, managing debt, and achieving financial independence. Each chapter is crafted to offer practical advice and tools that you can apply directly to your financial situation. My goal is to empower you to make informed decisions, develop a personalized financial plan, and ultimately achieve the financial stability and independence you desire.

Beyond the technical aspects of finance, this book also emphasizes the importance of developing a healthy money mindset. I believe that a positive and proactive approach to money management can significantly impact your overall well-being and success. By focusing on your own financial journey and aligning your goals with your values, you can create a fulfilling and secure financial future.

As you read through "Mind Your Own Money," I encourage you to reflect on your own financial goals and aspirations. Use the tools and strategies provided to create a plan that works for you and remember that managing your money is a dynamic process. Your financial journey is unique, and staying focused on your own path will help you achieve lasting success.

Thank you for joining me on this journey. I hope that the insights and advice shared in this book will inspire and guide you as you work towards a brighter financial future.

Warm regards,

Alphonso Horton

Introduction

Why Personal Finance is Personal

Personal finance is inherently personal because it is deeply intertwined with our individual values, goals, and circumstances. Unlike standardized financial advice or one-size-fits-all strategies, personal finance must reflect the unique aspects of each person's life. What works for one person might not work for another, and that's why understanding your own financial landscape is crucial.

Personal finance encompasses everything from budgeting and saving to investing and debt management. It is influenced by a variety of factors, including your income, expenses, financial goals, family situation, and even your mindset about money. Each individual's financial journey is shaped by their specific needs and aspirations, making it essential to tailor financial strategies to fit your own situation.

The Importance of Focusing on Your Own Financial Journey

In a world where social media and societal expectations often highlight the financial successes and lifestyles of others, it's easy to become distracted or disheartened. The pressure to "keep up with the Joneses" can lead to unnecessary spending, financial stress, and deviation from your own financial goals.

Focusing on your own financial journey involves concentrating on what matters most to you —your personal goals, values, and financial well-being. It means creating a budget that aligns with your needs, setting goals that reflect your aspirations, and making financial decisions that are best for you, not based on what others are doing.

By prioritizing your own financial path, you can achieve greater clarity, control, and satisfaction in your financial life. This approach allows you to make informed decisions, stay committed to your budget, and work towards goals that genuinely reflect your personal ambitions. Remember, financial success is not measured by comparing yourself to others but by achieving what you set out to accomplish for yourself.

Chapter 1: The Comparison Trap

How Comparing Yourself to Others Can Derail Your Financial Goals

In today's hyper-connected world, it's nearly impossible to avoid comparisons. Social media platforms, advertisements, and even casual conversations can constantly present a curated image of other people's financial success. It's easy to look at others' seemingly perfect lives and feel the urge to measure up. However, this comparison can be detrimental to your financial health.

When you focus on what others have, you might find yourself making financial decisions based on external appearances rather than your own needs and goals. The pressure to maintain a certain lifestyle or to match others' spending habits can lead to unnecessary expenses, debt accumulation, and ultimately, a detour from your financial objectives.

For example, if you see friends frequently dining out or upgrading their homes, you might feel compelled to do the same, even if it means stretching your budget or going into debt. This external pressure can cloud your judgment, leading to decisions that are inconsistent with your financial goals and values.

The Psychology Behind Envy and Financial Insecurity

The psychological effects of comparing yourself to others are complex and can significantly impact your financial behavior. Envy, a natural human emotion, can arise when you perceive that others have something you desire or believe they are better off financially. This feeling of inadequacy can create a sense of financial insecurity, pushing you to take actions that aren't aligned with your best interests.

Financial insecurity often leads to a cycle of stress and reactive behavior. When you compare yourself to others, you might feel a temporary boost of motivation to spend or invest in ways that aren't sustainable. However, this can also trigger a fear of falling behind, causing you to make hasty decisions or engage in impulsive spending to keep up appearances.

Understanding the psychology behind these emotions can help you recognize when you're falling into the comparison trap. It's important to address these feelings and shift your focus from external benchmarks to internal values and goals. By doing so, you can better manage your finances and make decisions that reflect your personal financial well-being.

Case Studies: The Hidden Costs of Keeping Up with the Joneses

1. Case Study: Sarah and the Lifestyle Inflation

    Sarah noticed that many of her colleagues were driving new cars and living in upscale neighborhoods. Feeling the pressure to fit in, she upgraded her car and moved to a more expensive apartment. While this seemed like a step up at first, Sarah soon found herself struggling with increased monthly payments and rising debt. The stress of maintaining her new lifestyle led her to cut back on savings and investments, ultimately derailing her long-term financial goals.

2. Case Study: Mark's Social Media Spending

    Mark frequently saw images of extravagant vacations and luxury purchases from friends on social media. Influenced by these posts, he began spending more on dining out and travel to appear as successful as his peers. This shift in spending habits quickly depleted his savings and led to significant credit card debt. The immediate gratification of keeping up with appearances came at the cost of financial stability and peace of mind.

3. Case Study: Lisa's Career and Financial Pressure

Lisa worked in a high-pressure job where her peers often flaunted their latest tech gadgets and designer clothing. In an attempt to fit in and gain social approval, Lisa started spending beyond her means on luxury items and high-end experiences. Despite earning a good salary, her financial health deteriorated as she prioritized her image over practical financial management, resulting in mounting debt and a lack of savings.

These case studies illustrate how the comparison trap can lead to poor financial decisions and long-term consequences. They highlight the importance of focusing on your own financial goals and making decisions based on your personal circumstances rather than external pressures. By understanding the hidden costs of keeping up with others, you can better navigate your financial journey and prioritize what truly matters to you.

Chapter 2: Understanding Your Unique Financial Landscape

Assessing Your Income, Expenses, and Financial Goals

Before you can effectively manage your finances, it is crucial to have a clear picture of your current financial situation. This involves a thorough assessment of your income, expenses, and financial goals.

1. Assessing Your Income

Start by identifying all sources of income. This includes your salary, any bonuses, rental income, investments, and any side gigs. It is important to calculate your net income, which is the amount you take home after taxes and other deductions. A comprehensive understanding of your total income will help you make informed budgeting and saving decisions.

2. Tracking Your Expenses

Next, take stock of your monthly expenses. Categorize them into fixed expenses (like rent or mortgage, utilities, insurance) and variable expenses (such as groceries, dining out, and entertainment). Tracking your expenses can be done through financial apps, spreadsheets, or even manually recording them. Understanding where your money goes each month helps you identify areas where you might be overspending or could potentially save.

3. Identifying Your Financial Goals

Financial goals can range from short-term objectives (such as saving for a vacation) to long-term aspirations (like retirement planning or buying a home). Clearly define your financial goals and prioritize them based on their importance and timeframe. Setting clear goals gives you direction and helps you create a financial plan that aligns with your priorities.

How to Create a Personal Financial Statement

A personal financial statement provides a snapshot of your financial health at a specific point in time. It consists of two main components: a balance sheet and an income statement.

1. Creating a Balance Sheet
   - Assets: List all your assets, including cash, investments, real estate, and personal property. Assign a current value to each asset.
   - Liabilities: List all your liabilities, such as credit card debt, student loans, mortgages, and car loans. Include the remaining balance on each debt.

- Net Worth: Subtract your total liabilities from your total assets to calculate your net worth. This figure represents your overall financial position.

2. Creating an Income Statement
   - Income: Record all sources of income, as discussed previously.
   - Expenses: List all monthly expenses, both fixed and variable.
   - Surplus/Deficit: Subtract your total expenses from your total income to determine whether you have a surplus (positive balance) or deficit (negative balance). This calculation helps you assess your cash flow and identify areas for improvement.

Regularly updating your personal financial statement allows you to monitor your financial progress and make necessary adjustments to stay on track with your goals.

Setting Realistic Financial Goals Based on Your Situation

Setting realistic financial goals is essential for achieving long-term financial success. Here is how to set goals that are both achievable and motivating:

1. Assess Your Current Situation
   Take into account your income, expenses, and net worth. Consider any existing debts, savings, and investments. Your current financial situation will help you determine what is realistic and achievable.

2. Define Specific Goals
   Clearly articulate your goals with specific details. Instead of a vague goal like "save more money," set a specific target such as "save $5,000 for an emergency fund within the next 12 months." Specific goals are easier to measure and achieve.

3. Set a Timeline

Establish a timeline for achieving each goal. Short-term goals might be achievable within a few months, while long-term goals could take several years. A timeline helps you stay focused and track your progress.

4. Break Down Goals into Actionable Steps

Divide larger goals into smaller, manageable steps. For example, if your goal is to save for a down payment on a house, break it down into monthly savings targets. This approach makes it easier to track progress and stay motivated.

5. Review and Adjust Regularly

Regularly review your financial goals and progress. Life circumstances and financial situations can change, so be prepared to adjust your goals and plans as needed. Flexibility ensures that your goals remain relevant and attainable.

By understanding your financial landscape, creating a detailed personal financial statement, and setting realistic goals, you lay the foundation for a well-structured financial plan. This approach helps you manage your money effectively, make informed decisions, and work towards achieving your financial aspirations.

Chapter 3: Building and Sticking to a Budget

The Basics of Budgeting: Creating a Simple, Effective Budget

Budgeting is the cornerstone of financial management. A well-constructed budget helps you track your income and expenses, ensuring that you live within your means and work towards your financial goals. Here's how to create a simple, effective budget:

1. Calculate Your Total Income

Begin by determining your total monthly income. This includes your salary, any side income, rental income, and any other sources of revenue. Make sure to use your net income—the amount you receive after taxes and other deductions.

2. List Your Monthly Expenses

Categorize your expenses into two main groups:

- Fixed Expenses: These are recurring costs that don't change much month-to-month, such as rent or mortgage, utilities, insurance premiums, and loan payments.

- Variable Expenses: These include costs that can fluctuate, such as groceries, dining out, entertainment, and transportation.

Keep track of these expenses for a month or two to get a clear picture of your spending patterns.

3. Set Budget Limits

Allocate specific amounts for each expense category based on your income. Start with essential expenses like housing and utilities, then allocate funds for discretionary spending. Make sure your total expenses do not exceed your total income.

4. Include Savings and Debt Repayment

Allocate a portion of your budget for savings and debt repayment. Prioritize building an emergency fund, contributing to retirement accounts, and paying down high-interest debt. Treat these contributions as non-negotiable expenses.

5. Monitor and Adjust

Track your spending against your budget throughout the month. If you find that you're consistently overspending in certain areas, adjust your budget or spending habits accordingly. Flexibility is key to maintaining a realistic and effective budget.

Tools and Apps to Help Manage Your Budget

Modern technology offers a variety of tools and apps that can simplify budgeting and help you stay on track:

1. Mint

Mint is a popular budgeting app that connects to your bank accounts and automatically categorizes your transactions. It provides a comprehensive overview of your finances, tracks your spending, and offers budgeting tools and alerts.

2. YNAB (You Need a Budget)

YNAB is designed to help you allocate every dollar you earn to specific expenses or savings goals. It emphasizes proactive budgeting and offers educational resources to improve your financial habits.

3. EveryDollar

EveryDollar, created by financial expert Dave Ramsey, offers a straightforward approach to budgeting. You can create and manage your budget easily, and it integrates with your bank accounts to track your spending.

4. PocketGuard

PocketGuard helps you understand how much disposable income you have after accounting for bills, goals, and necessities. It simplifies budgeting by showing you how much you can spend without jeopardizing your financial goals.

5. GoodBudget

GoodBudget is a digital envelope budgeting app that lets you allocate funds to different spending categories. It's ideal for those who prefer a traditional envelope budgeting system but want the convenience of digital tracking.

Strategies for Sticking to Your Budget

Creating a budget is just the first step; sticking to it requires discipline and strategic planning. Here are some effective strategies to help you adhere to your budget:

1. Automate Savings and Bill Payments

Set up automatic transfers to savings accounts and automatic payments for bills to ensure that you stay consistent with your savings goals and avoid late fees. Automating these transactions reduces the temptation to spend the money elsewhere.

2. Use Cash for Variable Expenses

Consider using cash for discretionary spending categories like dining out or entertainment. By withdrawing a set amount each month and using only that cash, you can better control your spending and avoid overspending.

3. Review and Adjust Regularly

Periodically review your budget to ensure it reflects any changes in your income, expenses, or financial goals. Adjust your budget as needed to stay on track and accommodate any significant life changes.

4. Track Your Spending

Keep a daily or weekly record of your expenses to stay mindful of your spending habits. Many budgeting apps provide real-time tracking, making it easier to monitor your expenses and make adjustments as needed.

5. Avoid Impulse Purchases
Implement strategies to resist impulse buying, such as creating a shopping list before going to the store, avoiding online shopping when you're bored, or waiting 24 hours before making a non-essential purchase.

6. Set Up a Reward System
Motivate yourself by setting up small rewards for sticking to your budget. For example, if you stay within your budget for a month, treat yourself to a small, planned indulgence. Rewards can make the budgeting process more enjoyable and sustainable.

7. Seek Support and Accountability
Share your budgeting goals with a trusted friend or family member who can provide encouragement and hold you accountable. Having someone to share your progress with can help you stay motivated and committed to your budget.

By understanding the basics of budgeting, leveraging helpful tools and apps, and employing effective strategies, you can build and maintain a budget that supports your financial goals and ensures long-term financial stability.

Chapter 4: Smart Spending: Prioritizing Needs vs. Wants

Identifying Essential Expenses vs. Discretionary Spending

Effective budgeting and financial management hinge on distinguishing between essential expenses and discretionary spending. Understanding this distinction helps you allocate your resources wisely and make informed spending decisions.

1. Essential Expenses

Essential expenses are necessary for maintaining your basic well-being and financial stability. These include:
- Housing: Rent or mortgage payments, property taxes, and homeowners' insurance.
- Utilities: Electricity, water, gas, and heating costs.
- Food: Groceries and necessary household supplies.
- Transportation: Car payments, fuel, public transportation costs, and insurance.
- Healthcare: Medical insurance premiums, prescriptions, and necessary medical treatments.
- Education: Tuition fees, textbooks, and other educational expenses.
- Minimum Debt Payments: Payments towards credit cards and loans to avoid penalties and accruing interest.

Essential expenses are non-negotiable and should be prioritized in your budget to ensure your basic needs are met.

2. Discretionary Spending

Discretionary spending, on the other hand, is non-essential and often related to personal preferences and lifestyle choices. Examples include:
- Dining Out: Meals at restaurants, cafes, and takeout.
- Entertainment: Movie tickets, concerts, hobbies, and recreational activities.
- Luxury Items: Designer clothing, high-end gadgets, and accessories.
- Vacations: Travel and leisure expenses.
- Subscriptions: Streaming services, magazines, and gym memberships.

While discretionary spending can enhance your quality of life, it should be managed carefully to avoid undermining your financial stability and goals.

The Importance of Mindful Spending

Mindful spending involves making deliberate and thoughtful financial decisions that align with your values and long-term goals. It contrasts with impulsive or automatic spending habits, which can lead to overspending and financial stress.

1. Assessing Value and Necessity

Before making a purchase, ask yourself if the item or service aligns with your financial goals and if it adds genuine value to your life. Consider whether the expense supports your long-term objectives or if it's a temporary indulgence.

2. Setting Spending Limits

Establishing spending limits for discretionary categories helps you control your expenses and prioritize essential needs. Stick to these limits to maintain financial discipline and avoid overextending your budget.

3. Aligning with Financial Goals

Ensure that your spending habits support your financial goals, such as saving for a down payment, paying off debt, or building an emergency fund. Mindful spending involves making choices that contribute to achieving these goals rather than detracting from them.

4. Avoiding Emotional Spending

Emotional spending occurs when you make purchases in response to stress, boredom, or other emotions rather than necessity. Recognize emotional triggers and find healthier ways to cope with feelings without resorting to spending.

Techniques for Avoiding Impulse Purchases

Impulse purchases can derail your budget and financial plans. Employing strategies to curb these spontaneous buying tendencies can help you stay on track with your financial goals.

1. Create a Shopping List and Stick to It

Before shopping, make a list of the items you need and commit to buying only what's on the list. This practice helps prevent impulse buys and keeps you focused on essential items.

2. Implement a 24-Hour Rule

For non-essential purchases, implement a 24-hour rule: wait at least 24 hours before making a decision. This cooling-off period allows you to reconsider the purchase and evaluate whether it's absolutely necessary.

3. Avoid Tempting Situations

Minimize exposure to situations that trigger impulse buying. Avoid browsing online shopping sites when you're bored or stressed and stay away from stores that you find particularly tempting.

4. Set Spending Limits

Establish a monthly or weekly spending limit for discretionary purchases. Use cash or a separate account for these expenses to make it easier to track and control your spending.

5. Unsubscribe from Marketing Emails

Unsubscribe from promotional emails and newsletters that may entice you to make impulse purchases. Reducing exposure to marketing messages helps you stay focused on your budget and financial goals.

6. Use a "Needs vs. Wants" Checklist

Create a checklist that categorizes potential purchases as "needs" or "wants." Evaluate each purchase against this checklist to determine if it aligns with your priorities and budget.

7. Find Alternatives to Spending

Discover alternative activities that don't involve spending money, such as exercising, reading, or spending time with friends. Engaging in these activities can fulfill your needs for entertainment and relaxation without impacting your budget.

By distinguishing between essential and discretionary spending, practicing mindful spending, and employing techniques to avoid impulse purchases, you can make more informed financial decisions. This approach helps you maintain control over your finances, prioritize your needs, and work towards your long-term financial goals.

Chapter 5: Saving for the Future

Building an Emergency Fund: Why and How

An emergency fund is a crucial component of a solid financial foundation. It provides a financial safety net for unexpected expenses and helps you avoid going into debt during emergencies. Here's why you need one and how to build it:

1. Why You Need an Emergency Fund
   - Unexpected Expenses: Emergencies such as medical bills, car repairs, or job loss can arise at any time. An emergency fund helps you cover these costs without derailing your budget or relying on credit.
   - Financial Stability: Having an emergency fund provides peace of mind and reduces financial stress, knowing that you have a cushion to fall back on in times of need.

- Avoiding Debt: With an emergency fund, you can avoid taking on high-interest debt to cover unexpected expenses, helping you maintain financial stability.

2. How to Build an Emergency Fund
   - Determine Your Target Amount: A common recommendation is to save three to six months' worth of living expenses. Calculate your monthly expenses and aim to build a fund that covers this amount.
   - Open a Separate Savings Account: Keep your emergency fund in a separate, easily accessible savings account. This ensures that the money is available when needed and reduces the temptation to dip into it for non-emergencies. Make sure its an high interest bearing account.
   - Set Up Automatic Transfers: Establish automatic transfers from your checking account to your emergency fund. Even small, regular contributions can add up over time.
   - Cut Unnecessary Expenses: To accelerate your savings, identify and cut non-essential expenses from your budget. Redirect these funds to your emergency fund.
   - Monitor and Adjust: Periodically review your emergency fund to ensure it meets your needs. Adjust your savings contributions as your financial situation changes.

Strategies for Long-Term Savings and Investments

Long-term savings and investments are essential for achieving financial goals and securing your financial future. Here are some strategies to help you build wealth over time:

1. Set Long-Term Goals
Define your long-term financial goals, such as buying a home, funding your child's education, or building a retirement fund. Having clear goals helps you determine how much to save and invest.

2. Utilize Retirement Accounts

- 401(k) Plans: If your employer offers a 401(k) plan, contribute regularly and take advantage of any employer matching contributions. The money grows tax-deferred until retirement.
- Individual Retirement Accounts (IRAs): Consider opening a Traditional or Roth IRA for additional retirement savings. Contributions to a Traditional IRA may be tax-deductible, while Roth IRA contributions are made with after-tax dollars but offer tax-free withdrawals in retirement.

3. Diversify Your Investments

Diversification reduces risk by spreading your investments across different asset classes, such as stocks, bonds, and real estate. This strategy helps balance potential returns with the risk of loss.

- Stocks: Invest in individual stocks or stocks mutual funds for growth potential. Understand your risk tolerance and invest accordingly.
- Bonds: Bonds provide steady income and are generally less volatile than stocks. Consider bond funds or individual bonds for a more conservative investment approach.
- Real Estate: Real estate investments can provide rental income and potential appreciation. Evaluate the risks and benefits of investing in property.

4. Regularly Contribute to Investment Accounts

Make regular contributions to your investment accounts, even if they are small. Consistent investing, along with the power of compounding interest, helps grow your wealth over time.

5. Review and Rebalance Your Portfolio

Periodically review your investment portfolio to ensure it aligns with your goals and risk tolerance. Rebalance your portfolio by adjusting the allocation of assets to maintain your desired investment strategy.

Retirement Planning: Starting Early and Staying Consistent

Planning for retirement is essential for ensuring financial security in your later years. Starting early and maintaining consistency in your retirement savings can have a significant impact on your financial future.

1. Start Early

- Compound Interest: The earlier you start saving for retirement, the more you benefit from compound interest. Even small contributions can grow significantly over time.

- Longer Investment Horizon: Starting early gives you a longer investment horizon, allowing your investments to recover from market fluctuations and grow more steadily.

2. Set Retirement Savings Goals

Determine how much you need to save for retirement based on your desired lifestyle, anticipated expenses, and life expectancy. Use retirement calculators to estimate the amount required to achieve your goals.

3. Contribute Regularly

- Automate Contributions: Set up automatic contributions to your retirement accounts to ensure consistent saving. Automating your contributions helps you stay on track with your retirement goals.

- Increase Contributions Over Time: As your income increases or expenses decrease, consider increasing your retirement contributions. Even small increases can have a substantial impact on your retirement savings.

4. Take Advantage of Employer Benefits

Maximize contributions to employer-sponsored retirement plans, such as 401(k)s, especially if your employer offers matching contributions. This free money helps boost your retirement savings.

5. Review Your Retirement Plan

Regularly review your retirement plan to assess your progress and make adjustments as needed. Consider factors such as changes in income, lifestyle, and market conditions.

6. Seek Professional Advice

Consult with a financial advisor to develop a personalized retirement plan. An advisor can help you assess your retirement needs, recommend investment strategies, and provide guidance on achieving your financial goals.

By building an emergency fund, implementing effective savings and investment strategies, and starting early with retirement planning, you can secure your financial future and work towards achieving your long-term financial goals. Consistency and proactive management are key to building a strong financial foundation and ensuring a comfortable retirement.

Chapter 6: Navigating Debt and Credit

Understanding Different Types of Debt and Their Impact

Debt is a common aspect of financial life, but not all debt is created equal. Understanding the diverse types of debt and their potential impact on your financial health is crucial for effective management.

1. Types of Debt
 - Revolving Debt: This includes credit cards and lines of credit, where you have a credit limit and can borrow up to that limit. Interest is charged on the outstanding balance, and you can carry a balance month-to-month. High-interest rates make revolving debt particularly costly if not managed carefully.
 - Installment Debt: This type of debt is repaid in regular, fixed payments over a set period. Examples include personal loans, auto loans, and student loans. These debts often have lower interest rates compared to revolving debt and are structured with a clear repayment schedule.

- Secured Debt: Secured debt is backed by collateral, such as a mortgage or auto loan. If you fail to repay, the lender can seize the collateral to recover the outstanding amount. Secured debt typically has lower interest rates due to the reduced risk for lenders.

- Unsecured Debt: Unsecured debt is not backed by collateral, such as credit card debt or medical bills. Because there is no collateral, this type of debt often comes with higher interest rates and more significant consequences for missed payments.

2. Impact of Debt on Financial Health

- Interest Costs: The cost of debt can be substantial due to interest charges. High-interest debt, such as credit card debt, can quickly become unmanageable and hinder your financial progress.

- Credit Score: The amount of debt you carry, and your payment history affect your credit score. High levels of debt or missed payments can negatively impact your credit score, making it harder to secure favorable loan terms in the future.

- Financial Stress: Carrying significant debt can lead to financial stress and anxiety. It's important to manage debt effectively to maintain financial well-being and peace of mind.

Strategies for Managing and Reducing Debt

Effectively managing and reducing debt involves a combination of strategies to make debt repayment more manageable and less stressful.

1. Create a Debt Repayment Plan

- List All Debts: Begin by listing all your debts, including the balance, interest rate, and minimum payment for each. This will help you understand your total debt load and prioritize repayment.

- Choose a Repayment Strategy: Two common strategies are:

- Debt Snowball Method: Focus on paying off the smallest debt first while making minimum payments on larger debts. Once the smallest debt is paid off, move on to the next smallest. This method can provide motivational boosts as you see debts being eliminated.

- Debt Avalanche Method: Focus on paying off the debt with the highest interest rate first while making minimum payments on other debts. This method saves money on interest over time but may take longer to see progress.

2. Negotiate with Creditors
    - Lower Interest Rates: Contact your creditors to negotiate lower interest rates or better terms on your debt. They may be willing to accommodate if you have a good payment history or are experiencing financial hardship.
    - Payment Plans: If you're struggling to make payments, request a modified payment plan that fits your budget. Creditors may offer temporary relief or more manageable payment terms.

3. Consolidate Debt
    - Debt Consolidation Loan: Consider taking out a debt consolidation loan to combine multiple debts into a single loan with a lower interest rate. This can simplify payments and potentially reduce overall interest costs.
    - Balance Transfer Credit Card: Use a balance transfer credit card to move high-interest credit card debt to a card with a lower interest rate or a promotional 0% APR period. Be cautious of balance transfer fees and ensure you can pay off the balance before the promotional period ends.

4. Cut Unnecessary Expenses
    Identify and reduce non-essential expenses to free up additional funds for debt repayment. Redirect these savings towards paying off your debt more quickly.

5. Increase Your Income
    Look for opportunities to increase your income, such as taking a side job or freelancing. Extra income can accelerate debt repayment and help you achieve financial stability faster.

Building and Maintaining Good Credit

A strong credit score is essential for accessing favorable loan terms and financial products. Building and maintaining good credit involves several key practices:

1. Pay Your Bills on Time

Timely payments are the most significant factor affecting your credit score. Set up automatic payments or reminders to ensure you never miss a due date.

2. Keep Credit Utilization Low

Credit utilization is the ratio of your credit card balances to your credit limits. Aim to keep this ratio below 30%. Lower utilization demonstrates responsible credit management and positively impacts your credit score.

3. Monitor Your Credit Report

Regularly check your credit report for accuracy and to identify any potential issues. You are entitled to a free credit report from each of the three major credit bureaus (Equifax, Experian, and TransUnion) annually. Dispute any errors promptly to maintain a clean credit history.

4. Maintain a Healthy Credit Mix

A healthy credit mix includes a combination of revolving credit (like credit cards) and installment loans (such as mortgages or auto loans). A diverse credit portfolio can positively influence your credit score, as long as you manage all accounts responsibly.

5. Avoid Opening Too Many New Accounts

While it's important to establish credit, avoid opening too many new credit accounts in a short period. Multiple credit inquiries can temporarily lower your credit score and may be viewed as a sign of financial distress.

6. Keep Old Accounts Open

The length of your credit history affects your credit score. Keep older accounts open and use them occasionally to maintain a long credit history.

Closing old accounts can shorten your credit history and potentially reduce your credit score.

By understanding different types of debt, implementing effective debt management strategies, and focusing on building and maintaining good credit, you can navigate debt and credit with confidence. These practices contribute to better financial health and help you achieve your long-term financial goals.

Chapter 7: The Role of Financial Independence

What Does Financial Independence Mean for You?

Financial independence is a state where you have enough wealth to cover your living expenses without relying on active income from work. It represents the freedom to make choices based on your values and desires, rather than being driven solely by financial necessity. Here's how to define financial independence in a way that aligns with your personal goals and values:

1. Defining Your Own Financial Independence
 - Personal Goals: Consider what financial independence means to you personally. For some, it might mean retiring early, starting a business, traveling the world, or pursuing hobbies without financial constraints. Clarify your vision of financial independence to set a meaningful and achievable goal.
 - Lifestyle Considerations: Think about the lifestyle you want to maintain. This includes your desired standard of living, housing, healthcare, and leisure activities. Your definition of financial independence should align with the lifestyle you envision for yourself.
 - Financial Needs and Wants: Distinguish between your essential needs and discretionary wants. Understanding this distinction helps you set

realistic financial targets and create a plan that supports both your current and future aspirations.

2. Measuring Financial Independence
- Net Worth: Assess your net worth by calculating the difference between your assets (savings, investments, property) and liabilities (debts, loans). A positive net worth indicates a stronger financial position.
- Income Streams: Evaluate your income streams. Financial independence often involves having multiple sources of passive income, such as investments, rental properties, or business ventures that generate income without requiring active work.

Steps to Achieve Financial Independence

Achieving financial independence involves strategic planning, disciplined saving, and smart investing. Here's a step-by-step approach to help you work towards this goal:

1. Set Clear Financial Goals
- Define Your Targets: Establish specific, measurable, achievable, relevant, and time-bound (SMART) goals for financial independence. This might include saving a certain amount, reaching a specific net worth, or generating a particular level of passive income.
- Create a Roadmap: Develop a financial plan that outlines the steps needed to achieve your goals. This plan should include budgeting, saving, investing, and debt management strategies.

2. Build a Solid Financial Foundation
- Establish an Emergency Fund: Ensure you have a well-funded emergency fund to cover unexpected expenses and protect your financial stability.
- Pay Off High-Interest Debt: Prioritize paying off high-interest debt to free up more resources for saving and investing.

3. Increase Your Income

- Advance in Your Career: Seek opportunities for career advancement, additional training, or higher-paying roles to increase your earning potential.
- Explore Side Hustles: Consider side jobs or freelance work to supplement your income. Extra earnings can accelerate your progress towards financial independence.
- Invest Wisely: Invest in assets that generate passive income, such as stocks, bonds, rental properties, or business ventures. Smart investing can significantly enhance your wealth over time.

4. Live Below Your Means
- Budgeting and Saving: Create and stick to a budget that emphasizes saving and investing. Avoid lifestyle inflation by keeping your expenses in check as your income increases.
- Cut Unnecessary Expenses: Identify and eliminate non-essential expenses to boost your savings rate. Redirect these savings towards investments that contribute to your financial independence.

5. Plan for Long-Term Financial Security
- Retirement Accounts: Contribute regularly to retirement accounts such as 401(k)s, IRAs, or other tax-advantaged accounts. Take advantage of employer matches and tax benefits.
- Diversify Investments: Diversify your investment portfolio to manage risk and optimize returns. Consider a mix of stocks, bonds, real estate, and other investment vehicles.

6. Monitor and Adjust Your Plan
- Review Progress: Regularly review your financial progress and adjust your plan as needed. Monitor your investments, savings, and expenses to stay on track with your goals.
- Adapt to Life Changes: Be flexible and adapt your financial plan to life changes, such as marriage, family growth, or career shifts. Adjust your savings and investment strategies accordingly.

The Importance of Financial Education and Continuous Learning

Financial independence is not a static goal but an ongoing journey that requires continuous learning and adaptation. Staying informed and educated about personal finance and investment strategies is crucial for maintaining and growing your financial independence. Here's why financial education is essential:

1. Stay Updated on Financial Trends
   - Market Changes: Financial markets and economic conditions change over time. Staying informed about market trends, interest rates, and investment opportunities helps you make well-informed decisions.
   - Regulatory Updates: Financial regulations and tax laws can impact your financial strategy. Keeping up with regulatory changes ensures that you comply with legal requirements and take advantage of new opportunities.

2. Improve Financial Decision-Making
   - Informed Choices: Financial education equips you with the knowledge to make informed decisions about budgeting, saving, investing, and managing debt. Better decision-making enhances your financial stability and growth.
   - Risk Management: Understanding financial concepts helps you assess and manage risks effectively. This includes diversifying investments, protecting assets, and avoiding financial pitfalls.

3. Enhance Financial Skills
   - Investment Strategies: Learn about various investment strategies and asset classes to build a diversified portfolio that aligns with your goals and risk tolerance.
   - Tax Planning: Gain knowledge about tax planning strategies to optimize your tax situation and maximize your savings.

4. Adapt to Financial Challenges

- Problem-Solving: Financial education helps you develop problem-solving skills to navigate financial challenges, such as unexpected expenses or market downturns.

- Strategic Planning: Continuously learning allows you to adapt your financial plan and strategies in response to changing circumstances and new opportunities.

5. Foster a Growth Mindset
 - Continuous Improvement: Embrace a growth mindset by seeking out new knowledge and skills. This mindset encourages ongoing learning and improvement, leading to better financial outcomes.

By defining what financial independence means to you, following a structured plan to achieve it, and committing to continuous financial education, you can build a secure financial future and enjoy the freedom to pursue your personal goals. Financial independence is a journey that requires dedication, adaptability, and lifelong learning.

Chapter 8: Developing a Healthy Money Mindset

Overcoming Financial Stress and Anxiety

Financial stress and anxiety can be overwhelming, but developing strategies to manage these feelings is crucial for maintaining overall well-being and financial health. Here's how to tackle financial stress effectively:

1. Identify the Sources of Stress
 - Understand Triggers: Pinpoint specific financial situations or concerns that trigger stress. Common sources include debt, job insecurity, or unexpected expenses. Recognizing these triggers helps you address them more effectively.

- Evaluate Your Financial Situation: Take a comprehensive look at your financial health. Assess your income, expenses, debts, and savings to get a clear picture of your financial status.

2. Develop a Plan of Action
   - Create a Budget: Develop a detailed budget to manage your finances more effectively. A well-structured budget helps you track expenses, plan for savings, and reduce financial uncertainty.
   - Set Financial Goals: Establish short-term and long-term financial goals to give you direction and purpose. Achieving these goals can alleviate stress and provide a sense of accomplishment.

3. Practice Stress-Relief Techniques
   - Mindfulness and Relaxation: Engage in mindfulness practices, such as meditation or deep breathing exercises, to reduce stress. These techniques help calm your mind and provide clarity in financial decision-making.
   - Exercise and Healthy Living: Regular physical activity and a healthy lifestyle contribute to overall well-being and can help manage stress levels. Incorporate exercise, proper nutrition, and adequate sleep into your routine.

4. Seek Professional Help
   - Financial Counseling: Consult a financial advisor or counselor for expert guidance on managing your finances and developing effective strategies. Professional advice can provide clarity and help you create a structured plan.
   - Mental Health Support: If financial stress is significantly impacting your mental health, consider seeking support from a therapist or counselor. They can provide tools and strategies for managing anxiety and stress.

Cultivating a Positive Relationship with Money

Developing a positive relationship with money involves changing your mindset and behaviors to view money as a tool for achieving your goals rather than a source of stress. Here's how to cultivate this positive relationship:

1. Shift Your Perspective
   - View Money as a Resource: Understand that money is a resource that can help you achieve your goals, support your lifestyle, and provide security. Shift your perspective from seeing money as a source of anxiety to viewing it as a tool for empowerment.
   - Focus on Abundance: Embrace an abundance mindset, where you believe there are ample opportunities and resources available. This mindset encourages proactive financial planning and reduces feelings of scarcity.

2. Develop Healthy Financial Habits
   - Budgeting and Saving: Practice effective budgeting and saving techniques. Consistent financial habits create stability and confidence in managing your money.
   - Avoid Comparing: Resist comparing your financial situation with others. Focus on your own progress and achievements rather than measuring success against external benchmarks.

3. Set Meaningful Financial Goals
   - Align Goals with Values: Set financial goals that align with your personal values and priorities. Goals that reflect your true aspirations can motivate you and create a sense of purpose in managing your finances.
   - Celebrate Achievements: Acknowledge and celebrate your financial milestones and achievements. Recognizing your progress fosters a positive outlook and reinforces good financial behaviors.

4. Practice Financial Self-Compassion
   - Be Kind to Yourself: Avoid self-criticism or guilt related to financial decisions. Practice self-compassion and recognize that everyone makes mistakes. Focus on learning and growing from financial experiences.

The Role of Gratitude and Financial Mindfulness

Gratitude and mindfulness can play significant roles in developing a healthy money mindset. These practices help you appreciate what you have and make more intentional financial decisions.

1. Practice Gratitude
   - Recognize Abundance: Regularly acknowledge and appreciate the positive aspects of your financial situation, no matter how small. This practice helps shift your focus from what you lack to what you have.
   - Gratitude Journaling: Keep a gratitude journal where you record things you are thankful for, including financial aspects. This exercise fosters a positive outlook and helps you maintain perspective.

2. Embrace Financial Mindfulness
   - Be Present with Your Finances: Approach your financial activities with mindfulness by being fully present when budgeting, saving, or making spending decisions. This practice helps you make thoughtful choices and reduces impulsive behavior.
   - Mindful Spending: Before making a purchase, pause and reflect on whether the expense aligns with your values and goals. Mindful spending ensures that your financial decisions are deliberate and purposeful.

3. Reflect on Your Financial Journey
   - Regular Reviews: Periodically review your financial progress and reflect on your journey. Assess your achievements, challenges, and areas for improvement. Reflection helps you stay connected to your goals and motivates continued growth.
   - Learn from Experiences: Use past financial experiences as learning opportunities. Reflect on both successes and setbacks to gain insights and enhance your financial mindset.

By addressing financial stress, cultivating a positive relationship with money, and incorporating gratitude and mindfulness into your financial practices, you can develop a healthier money mindset. These strategies contribute to overall financial well-being and create a more balanced and fulfilling approach to managing your finances.

Chapter 9: Monitoring and Adjusting Your Financial Plan

Regularly Reviewing and Updating Your Budget

A budget is a dynamic tool that requires regular review and adjustment to remain effective. Consistent monitoring helps ensure your financial plan stays aligned with your goals and adapts to changes in your circumstances. Here's how to keep your budget in check:

1. Schedule Regular Reviews
   - Monthly Check-ins: Review your budget on a monthly basis to track your spending, savings, and overall financial performance. Monthly reviews help identify any discrepancies or areas where adjustments may be needed.
   - Quarterly Assessments: Conduct a more detailed assessment every quarter. Evaluate your progress towards financial goals, review changes in income or expenses, and adjust your budget accordingly.

2. Track Actual Spending vs. Budgeted Amounts
   - Monitor Expenses: Compare your actual spending against your budgeted amounts. Identify any categories where you're overspending or underspending and make necessary adjustments.
   - Adjust Categories: If you find that certain budget categories are consistently off, adjust your budget to better reflect your actual spending patterns. This helps create a more realistic and manageable budget.

3. Review Financial Goals

- Assess Progress: Evaluate your progress towards your financial goals. Determine whether you're on track to achieve short-term and long-term objectives.
- Adjust Goals: If needed, revise your goals based on changes in your financial situation or priorities. Ensure your budget aligns with any updated goals or timelines.

4. Update for Changes in Income or Expenses
- Income Fluctuations: Adjust your budget if there are changes in your income, such as a salary increase, bonus, or a new job. Allocate additional income to savings, debt repayment, or investments as appropriate.
- Expense Changes: Incorporate changes in your expenses, such as new bills, changes in living costs, or major purchases. Update your budget to reflect these changes and maintain financial balance.

Adapting to Life Changes and Financial Shifts

Life events and financial shifts can significantly impact your financial situation and necessitate adjustments to your plan. Being proactive in adapting to these changes helps ensure continued financial stability and progress.

1. Recognize Major Life Events
- Marriage or Divorce: Significant life events such as marriage or divorce can impact your finances. Update your budget to reflect changes in income, expenses, and financial responsibilities.
- Family Growth: Having a child or other family changes require adjustments in your budget for increased expenses such as childcare, education, or healthcare.

2. Respond to Job Changes
- Career Advancement: A promotion or new job with a higher salary may necessitate changes in your budget. Reallocate additional income towards savings, investments, or debt reduction.

- Job Loss: In the event of job loss or reduced income, revisit your budget to prioritize essential expenses and explore ways to reduce non-essential spending.

3. Adjust for Economic Changes
   - Inflation: Rising inflation can impact your cost of living. Adjust your budget to account for increased prices on goods and services.
   - Interest Rates: Changes in interest rates can affect loan payments or investment returns. Update your budget to reflect any adjustments in interest rates on debts or savings accounts.

4. Plan for Major Purchases or Investments
   - Home or Vehicle Purchase: Major purchases require careful financial planning. Include savings goals for down payments and adjust your budget to accommodate new expenses such as mortgage or car payments.
   - Investments: When making significant investments, such as starting a business or purchasing real estate, ensure your budget accommodates these expenses and aligns with your financial goals.

When and How to Seek Professional Financial Advice

Seeking professional financial advice can provide valuable insights and guidance, especially during complex financial situations or significant life changes. Here's when and how to engage a financial advisor:

1. When to Seek Professional Advice
   - Complex Financial Situations: If you have complex financial needs, such as managing multiple investments, planning for retirement, or navigating tax strategies, professional advice can provide clarity and expertise.
   - Major Life Changes: During major life events, such as marriage, divorce, or career changes, a financial advisor can help you adjust your financial plan and navigate new financial responsibilities.

- Debt Management Issues: If you're struggling with debt or need a structured plan for debt repayment, a financial advisor can help create a strategy to manage and reduce debt effectively.

- Investment Decisions: When making significant investment decisions or planning for long-term financial goals, professional advice can help you make informed choices and optimize your investment strategy.

2. How to Choose a Financial Advisor

- Credentials and Experience: Look for a financial advisor with relevant credentials, such as Certified Financial Planner (CFP) or Chartered Financial Analyst (CFA), and experience in areas relevant to your financial needs.

- Specialization: Choose an advisor who specializes in the areas you need assistance with, such as retirement planning, tax strategies, or investment management.

- Fee Structure: Understand the advisor's fee structure, whether it's a flat fee, hourly rate, or commission-based. Ensure that their compensation aligns with your budget and that there are no conflicts of interest.

3. Prepare for Your First Meeting

- Gather Financial Information: Prepare a comprehensive overview of your financial situation, including income, expenses, assets, liabilities, and financial goals. This information will help the advisor provide tailored recommendations.

- Define Your Goals: Clearly articulate your financial goals and objectives. Discuss your priorities and any specific concerns or questions you have.

4. Review and Implement Recommendations

- Evaluate Advice: Review the advisor's recommendations carefully and ensure they align with your financial goals and values. Ask questions if anything is unclear.

- Implement Changes: Follow through with the advisor's recommendations and implement changes to your financial plan. Regularly review your progress and schedule follow-up meetings as needed.

By regularly reviewing and updating your budget, adapting to life changes and financial shifts, and seeking professional advice, when necessary, you can effectively manage and adjust your financial plan. These practices help ensure that your financial plan remains aligned with your goals and adapts to evolving circumstances, leading to greater financial stability and success.

Conclusion: Embracing Your Financial Journey

Embracing Your Financial Journey

Navigating your financial journey is a deeply personal endeavor that requires a blend of planning, patience, and adaptability. As you've explored throughout this book, managing your finances isn't just about numbers; it's about understanding your values, setting meaningful goals, and making informed decisions that align with your vision for the future.

1. Celebrate Your Progress: Acknowledge and celebrate the milestones you achieve along the way. Whether it's sticking to your budget, paying off debt, or reaching a savings goal, recognizing your successes reinforces positive habits and motivates continued effort.

2. Embrace Flexibility: Financial planning is not a static process. Life is unpredictable, and your financial plan should be adaptable. Embrace the journey with flexibility and openness to change, adjusting your strategies as needed to stay on track with your evolving goals.

3. Reflect and Learn: Regularly reflect on your financial journey and learn from your experiences. Every decision, success, and challenge offer valuable insights that contribute to your growth and understanding of money management.

Staying Focused on Your Own Goals and Values

In a world full of financial comparisons and external pressures, it's crucial to remain focused on your own goals and values. Your financial journey is unique, and staying true to your personal aspirations ensures that your financial decisions align with what truly matters to you.

1. Prioritize Your Values: Let your values guide your financial decisions. Whether it's saving for a dream vacation, investing in your education, or contributing to a cause you care about, align your financial choices with your core values.

2. Set Personal Goals: Define and pursue financial goals that are meaningful to you. Avoid the trap of comparing your progress to others; instead, measure success by how well you achieve your own objectives and fulfill your personal vision.

3. Practice Self-Compassion: Be kind to yourself throughout your financial journey. Understand that setbacks and challenges are part of the process. Practice self-compassion and focus on continuous improvement rather than perfection.

The Rewards of Mindful Money Management

Mindful money management brings numerous rewards beyond just financial stability. By approaching your finances with intention and awareness, you create a more balanced and fulfilling life.

1. Achieve Financial Freedom: Effective money management helps you achieve financial independence, providing the freedom to make choices based on your desires and priorities rather than financial constraints.

2. Reduce Financial Stress: By creating and following a well-structured financial plan, you reduce anxiety and stress related to money. This leads to greater peace of mind and overall well-being.

3. Enhance Your Quality of Life: Mindful money management allows you to enjoy the things that matter most to you, whether it's spending time with loved ones, pursuing hobbies, or achieving long-term dreams. Financial stability enhances your quality of life and enables you to live in alignment with your values.

4. Foster Long-Term Success: The habits and principles of mindful money management contribute to long-term financial success. By staying focused on your goals, regularly reviewing and adjusting your plan, and continually learning, you build a solid foundation for future prosperity.

In conclusion, embracing your financial journey with intention and mindfulness leads to a more fulfilling and secure financial future. By staying true to your goals and values, adapting to changes, and practicing mindful money management, you unlock the rewards of financial freedom, reduced stress, and a richer quality of life. Your financial journey is a personal and evolving process, and with the right mindset and strategies, you can navigate it with confidence and purpose.

Appendices

Appendix A: Budgeting Templates and Worksheets

To help you get started with managing your finances, we've included several budgeting templates and worksheets. These tools are designed to simplify the process of tracking income, expenses, and financial goals.

1. Monthly Budget Template

- Income: List all sources of income, including salary, bonuses, and other earnings.
- Fixed Expenses: Include rent/mortgage, utilities, insurance, and any other regular monthly payments.
- Variable Expenses: Track groceries, transportation, entertainment, and other variable costs.
- Savings and Investments: Record contributions to savings accounts, retirement funds, and other investments.
- Debt Repayment: Note any payments towards loans or credit card debt.
- Summary: Calculate total income, total expenses, and net savings.

2. Expense Tracking Worksheet
- Date: Record the date of each expense.
- Category: Classify each expense (e.g., dining, transportation, medical).
- Amount: Note the amount spent.
- Payment Method: Indicate whether the expense was paid in cash, credit, or debit.
- Notes: Add any relevant notes or comments.

3. Annual Financial Planner
- Income Projections: Estimate your annual income from all sources.
- Annual Expenses: Forecast your expected annual expenses, including seasonal or irregular costs.
- Savings Goals: Set annual savings targets for emergency funds, retirement, and other goals.
- Investment Strategy: Outline your planned investment contributions and strategies.
- Review Schedule: Plan regular review dates to track progress and adjust as needed.

Appendix B: Recommended Financial Tools and Resources

Here are some recommended tools and resources to help you manage your finances more effectively:

1. Budgeting Apps
   - Mint: A popular app for tracking spending, creating budgets, and monitoring financial goals.
   - YNAB (You Need A Budget): Focuses on helping users allocate every dollar to a specific purpose and adjust as needed.
   - EveryDollar: Simple budgeting tool that helps you create and stick to a monthly budget.

2. Expense Tracking Tools
   - Expensify: Streamlines expense tracking and reporting with receipt scanning and categorization features.
   - PocketGuard: Tracks your spending and shows how much disposable income you have after bills and goals are accounted for.

3. Investment Platforms
   - Robinhood: Provides commission-free trading for stocks, ETFs, and cryptocurrencies.
   - Vanguard: Offers a range of investment options, including mutual funds and ETFs, with a focus on low-cost investing.
   - Betterment: A robo-advisor that provides automated investment management based on your goals and risk tolerance.

4. Debt Management Tools
   - Credit Karma: Provides free credit scores and reports, along with tools to monitor and manage credit.
   - Debt Payoff Planner: Helps you create a plan to pay off debt using various strategies, such as the snowball or avalanche methods.

Appendix C: Additional Reading and Educational Resources

To further enhance your financial knowledge, consider exploring the following books and resources:

1. Books
   - "The Total Money Makeover" by Dave Ramsey: Offers a step-by-step plan for managing debt and building wealth.
   - "Your Money or Your Life" by Vicki Robin and Joe Dominguez: Provides insights into transforming your relationship with money and achieving financial independence.
   - "The Intelligent Investor" by Benjamin Graham: A classic guide to investing, focusing on value investing and long-term strategies.

2. Online Courses and Websites
   - Coursera: Offers courses on personal finance, budgeting, and investing from top universities and institutions.
   - Khan Academy: Provides free educational videos and tutorials on personal finance and economics.
   - Investopedia: A comprehensive resource for financial terms, investment strategies, and educational articles.

3. Podcasts and Blogs
   - "Earn Your Leisure": Explores a range of topics related to financial literacy, investing, and entrepreneurship, featuring interviews with experts and industry professionals.
   - "The Dave Ramsey Show": Provides practical financial advice and strategies for managing money and building wealth.
   - "ChooseFI": Focuses on financial independence and early retirement with actionable tips and personal stories.
   - "Mr. Money Mustache": A blog dedicated to frugality, financial independence, and living a fulfilling life with less.

By utilizing these tools, resources, and educational materials, you can enhance your financial management skills and continue to grow your financial knowledge. These appendices are designed to support you in implementing the principles discussed in this book and achieving your financial goals.

Glossary of Financial Terms

Navigating personal finance can be complex, but understanding key financial terms can greatly simplify the process. Here's a glossary of essential financial terms to help you better understand your financial journey:

1. Assets
   - Definition: Items of value owned by an individual or organization, such as cash, real estate, and investments.
   - Example: A home, stocks, and savings accounts.

2. Budget
   - Definition: A plan that outlines expected income and expenses over a specific period, typically monthly or annually.
   - Example: A monthly budget may include income from a salary and expenses like rent, groceries, and utilities.

3. Credit Score
   - Definition: A numerical representation of an individual's creditworthiness, typically ranging from 300 to 850.
   - Example: A higher credit score indicates better creditworthiness and can result in lower interest rates on loans.

4. Debt
   - Definition: Money borrowed that must be repaid, often with interest, such as loans or credit card balances.
   - Example: A mortgage, student loans, and credit card debt.

5. Emergency Fund

- Definition: Savings set aside to cover unexpected expenses or financial emergencies.
- Example: Funds reserved for medical emergencies or car repairs.

6. Expenses
   - Definition: The costs incurred for goods and services, including both fixed and variable expenses.
   - Example: Monthly rent (fixed expense) and dining out (variable expense).

7. Income
   - Definition: Money received from various sources, such as wages, salaries, investments, and other earnings.
   - Example: Salary from employment, dividends from stocks, and rental income.

8. Investment
   - Definition: An asset or item acquired with the expectation of generating future income or profit.
   - Example: Stocks, bonds, and real estate properties.

9. Net Worth
   - Definition: The difference between an individual's total assets and total liabilities (debts).
   - Example: If assets total $200,000 and liabilities are $150,000, the net worth is $50,000.

10. Savings Account
    - Definition: A bank account that earns interest on deposited funds and is used for saving money.
    - Example: A high-yield savings account that offers better interest rates compared to traditional savings accounts.

11. Interest Rate
    - Definition: The percentage charged or earned on borrowed or deposited funds.

- Example: The annual percentage rate (APR) on a loan or the interest earned on a savings account.

12. Retirement Plan
    - Definition: A financial plan designed to save and invest money for retirement, such as a 401(k) or IRA.
    - Example: Contributions to a 401(k) plan through an employer.

13. Diversification
    - Definition: The practice of spreading investments across various asset classes to reduce risk.
    - Example: Investing in a mix of stocks, bonds, and real estate.

14. Financial Independence
    - Definition: The state of having sufficient income and assets to cover living expenses without relying on employment.
    - Example: Achieving financial independence through careful saving and investing, allowing early retirement.

15. Credit Card
    - Definition: A plastic card issued by a financial institution allowing the holder to borrow funds for purchases up to a certain limit.
    - Example: Using a credit card to make purchases and paying off the balance to avoid interest charges.

16. Debt-to-Income Ratio
    - Definition: A measure of an individual's monthly debt payments relative to their monthly income.
    - Example: If monthly debt payments total $1,000 and monthly income is $4,000, the debt-to-income ratio is 25%.

17. Liquidity
    - Definition: The ease with which an asset can be converted into cash without significantly affecting its value.
    - Example: Cash and savings accounts are highly liquid, while real estate is less liquid.

18. Mutual Fund
   - Definition: An investment vehicle that pools funds from multiple investors to invest in a diversified portfolio of assets.
   - Example: A mutual fund that invests in a mix of stocks and bonds.

19. Stocks
   - Definition: Shares representing ownership in a corporation, entitling the holder to a portion of the company's profits.
   - Example: Purchasing shares of Apple Inc. through the stock market.

20. Bonds
   - Definition: Debt securities issued by corporations or governments that pay interest over time and return the principal at maturity.
   - Example: U.S. Treasury bonds or corporate bonds from large companies.

21. Expense Ratio
   - Definition: The percentage of a mutual fund's assets used for operating expenses, excluding brokerage fees.
   - Example: A mutual fund with a 1% expense ratio charges $1 annually for every $100 invested.

22. Tax-Advantaged Accounts
   - Definition: Accounts that provide tax benefits, such as tax deductions or tax-free growth, to encourage saving and investing.
   - Example: Individual Retirement Accounts (IRAs) and Health Savings Accounts (HSAs).

23. Compound Interest
   - Definition: Interest calculated on the initial principal and also on the accumulated interest from previous periods.
   - Example: Earning interest on both your initial savings and the interest previously earned.

24. Annual Percentage Rate (APR)

- Definition: The yearly interest rate charged on borrowed funds, expressed as a percentage.

- Example: An APR of 5% on a loan means you pay 5% of the loan amount in interest each year.

25. 401(k)

- Definition: A retirement savings plan offered by employers that allows employees to save and invest for retirement with tax advantages.

- Example: Contributing a portion of your salary to a 401(k) plan, with potential employer matching contributions.

Understanding these terms will help you make informed decisions, track your financial progress, and effectively manage your personal finances.

www.ingramcontent.com/pod-product-compliance
Lightning Source LLC
Chambersburg PA
CBHW072004210526
45479CB00003B/1054